Thomas Paine

The decline and fall of the English system of finance

Thomas Paine

The decline and fall of the English system of finance

ISBN/EAN: 9783337085780

Printed in Europe, USA, Canada, Australia, Japan

Cover: Foto ©Suzi / pixelio.de

More available books at **www.hansebooks.com**

THE
DECLINE

AND

FALL

OF THE

English System of Finance.

BY THOMAS PAINE,

AUTHOR OF COMMON SENSE, AMERICAN CRISIS,
RIGHTS OF MAN, AGE OF REASON, &c.

" On the verge, nay even in the gulph of bankruptcy."
Debates in Parliament.

PARIS:

PRINTED BY HARTLEY, ADLARD AND SON,
RUE NEUVE DE BERRY, NO. 5, AUX CHAMPS ELYSEES.
LONDON: REPRINTED FOR D. I. EATON, NO. 74, NEWGATE-
STREET.

1796.

ENTERED AT STATIONERS HALL.

DECLINE, &c.

NOTHING, they fay, is more certain that death, and nothing more uncertain than the time of dying; yet we can always fix a period beyond which man cannot live, and within fome moment of which he will die. We are enabled to do this, not by any fpirit of prophecy, or forefight into the event, but by obfervation of what has happened in all cafes of human or animal exiftence. If then any other fubject, fuch, for inftance, as a fyftem of finance, exhibits in its progrefs a feries of fymptoms indicating decay, its final diffolution is certain, and the period of it can be calculated from the fymptoms it exhibits.

'Thofe who have hitherto written on the Englifh fyftem of finance (the funding fyftem) have been

uniformly

uniformly impreſſed with the idea of its downfal happening *ſome time or other*. They took, however, no data for that opinion, but expreſſed it predictively, or merely as opinion, from a conviction that the perpetual duration of ſuch a ſyſtem was a natural impoſſibility. It is in this manner that Dr. Price has ſpoken of it; and Smith, in his Wealth of Nations, has ſpoken in the ſame manner; that is, merely as opinion without data. "The pro-"greſs," ſays Smith, "of the enormous debts, "which at preſent oppreſs, and will in the long-run "*moſt probably ruin*, all the great nations of Eu-"rope, (he ſhould have ſaid *governments*) has been "pretty uniform." But this general manner of ſpeaking, though it might make ſome impreſſion, carried with it no conviction.

It is not my intention to predict any thing; but I will ſhew from data already known, from ſymptoms and facts which the Engliſh funding ſyſtem has already exhibited publicly, that it will not continue to the end of Mr. Pitt's life, ſuppoſing him to live the uſual age of a man. How much ſooner it may fall, I leave to others to predict.

Let financiers diverſify ſyſtems of credit as they will, it is nevertheleſs true, that every ſyſtem of credit is a ſyſtem of paper money. Two experiments have already been had upon paper money; the one in America, the other in France. In both

thoſe

thofe cafes the whole capital was emitted, and that whole capital, which in America was called continental money, and in France affignats, appeared in circulation; the confequence of which was, that the quantity became fo enormous, and fo difproportioned to the quantity of population, and to the quantity of objeƈls upon which it could be employed, that the market, if I may fo exprefs it, was glutted with it, and the value of it fell. Between five and fix years determined the fate of thofe experiments. The fame fate would have happened to gold and filver, could gold and filver have been iffued in the fame abundant manner as paper had been, and confined within the country as paper money always is, by having no circulation out of it; or to fpeak on a larger fcale, the fame thing would happen in the world, could the world be glutted with gold and filver, as America and France has been with paper.

The Englifh fyftem differs from that of America and France in this one particular, that its capital is kept out of fight; that is, it does not appear in circulation. Were the whole capital of the national debt, which at the time I write this is almoft four hundred million pounds fterling, to be emitted in affignats or bills, and that whole quantity put into circulation, as was done in America and in France, thofe Englifh affignats, or bills, would fink in value

as thofe of America and France have done; and
that in a greater degree, becaufe the quantity of
them would be more difproportioned to the quantity of population in England, than was the cafe in
either of the other two countries. A nominal
pound fterling in fuch bills would not be worth one
penny.

But though the Englifh fyftem, by thus keeping the capital out of fight, is preferved from hafty
deftruction, as in the cafe of America and France,
it neverthelefs approaches the fame fate, and will
arrive at it with the fame certainty, though by a
flower progrefs. The difference is altogether in
the degree of fpeed by which the two fyftems approach their fate, which, to fpeak in round numbers, is as twenty is to one; that is, the Englifh
fyftem, that of funding the capital inftead of iffu-
ing it, contained within itfelf a capacity of endur-
ing twenty times longer than the fyftems adopted
by America and France; and at the end of that
time it would arrive at the fame common grave, the
Potter's field, of paper money.

The datum, I take for this proportion of twenty
to one, is the difference between a capital and the
intereft at five per cent. Twenty times the intereft is equal to the capital. The accumulation of
paper money in England is in proportion to the accumulation of the intereft upon every new loan;

and

and therefore the progrefs to diffolution is twenty times flower than if the capital were to be emitted and put into circulation immediately. Every twenty years in the Englifh fyftem is equal to one year in the French and American fyftems.

Having thus ftated the duration of the two fyftems, that of funding upon intereft, and that of emitting the whole capital without funding, to be as twenty to one, I come to examine the fymptoms of decay, approaching to diffolution, that the Englifh fyftem has already exhibited, and to compare them with fimilar fymptoms in the French and American fyftems.

The Englifh funding fyftem began one hundred years ago; in which time there has been fix wars, including the war that ended in 1697.

1. The war that ended, as I have juft faid, in 1697.
2. The war that began in 1702.
3. The war that began in 1739.
4. The war that began in 1756.
5. The American war, that began in 1775.
6. The prefent war, that began in 1793.

The national debt, at the conclufion of the war, which ended in 1697, was twenty-one millions and an half. (See Smith's Wealth of Nations, chapter on Public Debts. We now fee it approaching faft to four hundred millions. If be-

tween

tween thofe two extremes of twenty-one millions
and four hundred millions, embracing the feveral
expences of all the including wars, there exifts
fome common ratio that will afcertain arithmeti-
cally the amount of the debt at the end of each
war, as certainly as the fact is now known to be,
that ratio will in like manner determine what the
amount of the debt will be in all future wars,
and will afcertain the period within which the
funding fyftem will expire in a bankruptcy of
the government; for the ratio I allude to is the
ratio which the nature of the thing has eftablifhed
for itfelf.

Hitherto no idea has been entertained that any
fuch ratio exifted, or could exift, that could determine a problem of this kind, that is, that could
afcertain, without having any knowledge of the
fact, what the expence of any former war had
been, or what the expence of any future war would
be; but it is neverthelefs true that fuch a ratio
does exift, as I fhall fhew, and alfo the mode of
applying it.

The ratio I allude to is not in arithmetical progreffion, like the numbers

2, 3, 4, 5, 6, 7, 8, 9;

nor yet in geometrical progreffion, like the numbers

2, 4, 8, 16, 32, 64, 128, 256:

but

but is in the feries of one half upon each preceding number; like the numbers

8, 12, 18, 27, 40, 60, 90, 135.

Any perfon can perceive that the fecond number, 12, is produced by the preceding number, 8, and half 8; and that the third number, 18, is in like manner produced by the preceding number, 12, and half 12; and fo on for the reft. They can alfo fee how rapidly the fums increafe as the ratio proceeds. The difference between the two firft numbers is but four; but the difference between the two laft is forty-five: and from thence they may fee with what immenfe rapidity the national debt has increafed, and will continue to increafe, till it exceeds the ordinary powers of calculation, and lofes itfelf in cyphers.

I come now to apply the ratio as a rule to determine all the cafes.

I begin with the war that ended in 1697, which was the war in which the funding fyftem began. The expence of that war was twenty-one millions and an half. In order to afcertain the expence of the next war, I add to twenty-one millions and an half, the half thereof (ten millions and three quarters), which makes thirty-two millions and a quarter for the expence of that war. This thirty-two millions and a quarter, added to the former debt of twenty-one millions and an half,

B 4 carries

carries the national debt to fifty-three millions and three quarters. Smith, in his chapter on Public Debts, fays, The national debt was at this time fifty-three millions.

I proceed to afcertain the expence of the next war, that of 1739, by adding, as in the former cafe, one half to the expence of the preceding war. The expence of the preceding war was thirty-two millions and a quarter; for the fake of even numbers, fay thirty-two millions; the half of which (16) makes forty-eight millions for the expence of that war.

I proceed to afcertain the expence of the war of 1756, by adding, according to the ratio, one half to the expence of the preceding war. The expence of the preceding war was taken at 48 millions, the half of which (24) makes 72 millions for the expence of that war. Smith (chapter on Public Debts) fays, the expence of the war of 1756 was 72 millions and a quarter.

I proceed to afcertain the expence of the American war, of 1775, by adding, as in the former cafes, one half to the expence of the preceding war. The expence of the preceding war was 72 millions, the half of which (36) makes 108 millions for the expence of that war. In the laft edition of Smith (chapter on Public Debts) he fays, the expence

expence of the American war was *more than an hundred millions.*

I come now to afcertain the expence of the prefent war, fuppofing it to continue as long as former wars have done, and the funding fyftem not to break up before that period. The expence of the preceding war was 108 millions, the half of which (54) makes 162 millions for the expence of the prefent war. It gives fymptoms of going beyond this fum, fuppofing the funding fyftem not to break up; for the loans of the laft year and of the prefent year, are twenty-two millions each, which exceeds the ratio compared with the loans of the preceding war. It will not be from the inability of procuring loans that the fyftem will break up. On the contrary, it is the facility with which loans can be procured, that haftens that event. The loans are altogether paper tranfac-tions; and it is the excefs of them that brings on, with accelerating fpeed, that progreffive deprecia-tion of funded paper money that will diffolve the funding fyftem.

I proceed to afcertain the expence of future wars, and I do this merely to fhew the impoffibility of the continuance of the funding fyftem, and the certainty of its diffolution.

The

The expence of the next war after the prefent war, according to the ratio that has afcertained the preceding cafes will be —— 243 millions

Expence of the fecond war —— 364 millions

————————— third war —— 546 millions

————————— fourth war —— 819 millions

————————— fifth war —— 1228 millions

————

3200 millions

which, at only 4 per cent, will require taxes to the nominal amount of one hundred twenty-eight millions to pay the annual intereft, befides the intereft of the prefent debt, and the expences of government, which are not included in this account. Is there a man fo mad, fo ftupid, as to fuppofe this fyftem can continue?

When I firft conceived the idea of feeking for fome common ratio that fhould apply as a rule of meafurement to all the cafes of the funding fyftem, fo far as to afcertain the feveral ftages of its approach to diffolution, I had no expectation that any ratio could be found that would apply with fo much exactnefs as this does. I was led to the idea merely by obferving that the funding fyftem was a thing in continual progreffion, and that whatever was in a ftate of progreffion might be fuppofed to admit of, at leaft, fome general ratio of meafurement,

ment, that would apply without any very great variation. But who could have fuppofed that falling fyftems, or falling opinions, admitted of a ratio apparently as true as the defcent of falling bodies? I have not *made* the ratio, any more than Newton made the ratio of gravitation. I have only difcovered it, and explained the mode of applying it.

To fhew at one view the rapid progreffion of the funding fyftem to deftruction, and to expofe the folly of thofe who blindly believe in its continuance, or who artfully endeavor to impofe that belief upon others, I exhibit in the annexed table, the expence of each of the fix wars fince the funding fyftem began, as afcertained by the ratio, and the expence of fix wars yet to come, afcertained by the fame ratio,

First fix wars.				Second fix wars			
1	-	-	21 millions	1	-	-	243 millions
2	-	-	33 millions	2	-	-	364 millions
3	-	-	48 millions	3	-	-	546 millions
4	-	-	72 millions*	4	-	-	819 millions
5	-	-	108 millions	5	-	-	1228 millions
6	-	-	162 millions	6	-	-	1842 millions
Total	-	-	444 millions	Total	-	-	5042 millions

Thofe

* The actual expence of the war of 1739 did not come up to the fum afcertained by the ratio. But as that which is the natural difpofition of a thing, as it is the natural difpofition of a ftream of water to defcend, will, if impeded

in

Thofe who are acquainted with the power with which even a fmall ratio, acting in progreffion, multiplies in a long feries, will fee nothing to wonder at in this table. Thofe who are not acquainted with that fubject, and not knowing what elfe to fay, may be inclined to deny it. But it is not their opinion one way, nor mine the other, that can influence the event. The table exhibits the natural march of the funding fyftem to its irredeemable diffolution.—Suppofing the prefent government of England to continue, and to go on as it has gone on fince the funding fyftem began, I would not give twenty fhillings for one hundred pounds in the funds to be paid twenty years hence. I do not fpeak this predictively; I produce the data upon

in its courfe, overcome by a new effort what it had loft by that impediment, fo it was with refpect to this war and the next (1756), taken collectively; for the expence of the war 1756 reftored the equilibrium of the ratio, as fully as if it had not been impeded. A circumftance that ferves to prove the truth of the ratio more fully than if the interruption had not taken place. The war of 1739 was languid: the efforts were below the value of money at that time: for the ratio is the meafure of the depreciation of money in confequence of the funding fyftem; or what comes to the fame end, it is the meafure of the increafe of paper. Every additional quantity of it, whether in bank-notes or otherwife, diminifhes the *real*, though not the *nominal*, value of the former quantity.

which

which that belief is founded: and which data it is every body's intereſt to know, who have any thing to do with the funds, or who are going to bequeath property to their deſcendants to be paid at a future day.

Perhaps it may be aſked, that as governments or miniſters proceeded by no ratio in making loans or incurring debts, and as nobody intended any ratio, or thought of any, how does it happen that there is one? I anſwer, that the ratio is founded in neceſſity; and I now go to explain what that neceſſity is.

It will always happen, that the price of labor, or of the produce of labor, be that produce what it may, will be in proportion to the quantity of money in a country, admitting things to take their natural courſe. Before the invention of the funding ſyſtem, there was no other money than gold, and ſilver; and as nature gives out thoſe metals with a ſparing hand, and in regular annual quantities from the mines, the ſeveral prices of things were proportioned to the quantity of money at that time, and ſo nearly ſtationary as to vary but little in any fifty or ſixty years of that period.

When the funding ſyſtem began, a ſubſtitute for gold and ſilver began alſo. That ſubſtitute was paper; and the quantity of it increaſed as the quantity of intereſt increaſed upon accumulated loans.

loans. This appearance of a new and additional species of money in the nation soon began to break the relative value which money and the things it will purchase bore to each other before. Every thing rose in price; but the rise at first was little and slow, like the difference in units between the two first numbers, **8** and **12**, compared with the two last numbers, 90 and 135, in the table. It was however sufficient to make itself considerably felt in a large transaction. When therefore government, by engaging in a new war, required a new loan, it was obliged to make a higher loan than the former loan, to balance the increased price to which things had risen; and as that new loan increased the quantity of paper in proportion to the new quantity of interest, it carried the price of things still higher than before. The next loan was again higher, to balance that further increased price; and all this in the same manner, though not in the same degree, that every new emission of continental money in America, or of assignats in France, were greater than the preceding emission, to make head against the advance of prices, till the combat could be maintained no longer. Herein is founded the necessity of which I have just spoken. That necessity proceeds with accelerating velocity, and the ratio I have laid down is the measure of that acceleration; or, to speak the technical language

of

of the fubjeĉt, it is the meafure of the increafing depreciation of funded paper money, which it is impoffible to prevent, while the quantity of that money and of bank notes continues to multiply. What elfe but this can account for the difference between one war cofting 21 millions, and another war cofting 160 millions?

The difference cannot be accounted for on the fcore of extraordinary efforts or extraordinary atchievements. The war that coft 21 millions was the war of the confederates, hiftorically called the grand alliance, confifting of England, Auftria, and Holland, in the time of William the Third, againft Louis the Fourteenth, and in which the confederates were victorious. The prefent is a war of a much greater confederacy—a confederacy of England, Auftria, Pruffia, the German Empire, Spain, Holland, Naples, and Sardinia, eight powers againft the French Republic fingly, and the Republic has beaten the whole confederacy.—But to return to my fubjeĉt —

It is faid in England, that the value of paper keeps equal with the value of gold and filver. But the cafe is not rightly ftated; for the faĉt is, that the paper has *pulled down* the value of gold and filver to a level with itfelf. Gold and filver will not purchafe fo much of any purchafable article at this day as if no paper had appeared, nor fo

much

much as it will in any country in Europe where there is no paper. How long this hanging together of money and paper will continue makes a new cafe ; becaufe it daily expofes the fyftem to fudden death, independent of the natural death it would otherwife fuffer.

I confider the funding fyftem as being now advanced into the laft twenty years of its exiftence. The fingle circumftance, were there no other, that a war fhould now coft *nominally* one hundred and fixty millions, which when the fyftem began coft but twenty-one millions, or that the loan for one year only (including the loan to the Empeor) fhould now be *nominally* greater than the whole expence of that war, fhews the ftate of depreciation to which the funding fyftem has arrived. Its depreciation is in the proportion of eight for one, compared with the value of its money when the fyftem began; which is the ftate the French affignats ftood in a year ago (March, 1795), compared with gold and filver. It is therefore that I fay, that the Englifh funding fyftem, has entered into the laft twenty years of its exiftence, comparing each twenty years of the Englifh fyftem with every fingle year of the American and French fyftems, as before ftated.

Again, fuppofing the prefent war to clofe as former wars have done, and without producing either
revolu-

revolution or reform in England, another war, at least muft be looked for in the fpace of the twenty years I allude to; for it has never yet happened that twenty years have paffed off without a war, and that more efpecially fince the Englifh government has dabbled in German politics, and fhewn a difpofition to infult the world, and the world of commerce, with her navy. That next war will carry the national debt to very nearly feven hundred millions, the intereft of which, at four per cent, will be twenty-eight millions, befides the taxes for the (then) expences of government, which will increafe in the fame proportion, and which will carry the taxes to at leaft forty millions; and if another war only begins, it will quickly carry them to above fifty; for it is in the laft twenty years of the funding fyftem, as in the laft year of the American and French fyftems without funding, that all the great fhocks begin to operate.

I have juft mentioned that paper, in England, has *pulled down* the value of gold and filver to a level with itfelf; and that this *pulling down* of gold and filver money has created the appearance of paper money keeping up. The fame thing, and the fame miftake, took place in America and in France, and continued for a confiderable time after the commencement of their fyftem of paper; and

C   the

the actual depreciation of money was hidden under that miftake.

It was faid in America, at that time, that every thing was becoming *dear ;* but gold and filver could then buy thofe dear articles no cheaper than paper could; and therefore it was not called depreciation. The idea of *dearnefs* eftablifhed itfelf for the idea of depreciation. The fame was the cafe in France. Though every thing rofe in price foon after affignats appeared, yet thofe dear articles could be purchafed no cheaper with gold and filver than with paper, and it was only faid that things were *dear.* The fame is ftill the language in England. They call it *dearnefs.* But they will foon find that it is an actual depreciation, and that this depreciation is the effect of the funding fyftem; which, by crowding fuch a continually-increafing mafs of paper into circulation, carries down the value of gold and filver with it. But gold and filver will, in the long run, revolt againft depreciation, and feparate from the value of paper; for the progrefs of all fuch fyftems appears to be, that the paper will take the command in the beginning, and gold and filver in the end.

But this fucceffion in the command of gold and filver over paper, makes a crifis far more eventful to the funding fyftem than to any other fyftem upon which paper can be iffued; for, ftrictly speaking, it is not a crisis of danger, but a symptom of death. It is a death stroke to the funding system. It is a revolution in the whole of its affairs.

If paper be issued without being funded upon interest, emissions of it can be continued after the value of it separates from gold and silver, as we have seen in the two cases of America and France. But the funding system rests altogether upon the value of paper being equal to gold and silver; which will be as long as the paper can continue carrying down the value of gold and silver to the same level to which itself descends, and no longer. But even in this state, that of descending equally together, the minister, whoever he may be, will find himself beset with accumulating difficulties; because the loans and taxes voted for the service of each ensuing year will wither in his hands before the year expires, or before they can be applied. This will force him to have recourse to emissions of what are called exchequer and navy bills, which, by still increasing the mass of paper in circulation, will drive on the depreciation still more rapidly.

It ought to be known that taxes in England are not paid in gold and silver, but in paper (bank notes). Every person who pays any considerable quantity of taxes, such as maltsters, brewers, dis-

tillers

tillers (I appeal for the truth of it to any of the collectors of excife in England, or to Mr. Whitbread), knows this to be the cafe. There is not gold and filver enough in the nation to pay the taxes in coin, as I fhall fhew; and confequently there is not money enough in the bank to pay the notes. The intereft of the national funded debt is paid at the bank in the fame kind of paper in which the taxes are collected. When people find, as they will find, a refervednefs among each other in giving gold and filver for bank notes, or the leaft preference for the former over the latter, they will go for payment to the bank, where they have a right to go. They will do this as a meafure of prudence, each one for himfelf, and the truth or delufion of the funding fyftem will then be proved.

I have faid in the foregoing paragraph that there is not gold and filver enough in the nation to pay the taxes in coin, and confequently that there cannot be enough in the bank to pay the notes. As I do not chufe to reft any thing upon affertion, I appeal for the truth of this to the publications of Mr. Eden (now called Lord Auckland), and George Chalmers, Secretary to the Board of Trade and Plantation, of which Jenkinfon (now called Lord Hawkefbury) is prefident. [Thefe fort of folks change their names fo often, that it is as difficult to know them as it is to know a thief.] Chalmers gives the quantity of gold and filver coin from the returns of coinage at the mint; and, after deducting for the light gold recoined, fays, that the amount of gold and filver coin is *about twenty millions.* He had better not have proved this, especially if he had reflected, that *public credit is fufpicion afleep.* The quantity is much too little.

Of this twenty millions (which is not a fourth part of the quantity of gold and filver there is in France, as is fhewn in Mr. Necker's Treatife on the Adminiftration of the Finances) three millions at leaft muft be fuppofed to be in Ireland, fome in Scotland, and in the Weft Indies, Newfoundland, &c. The quantity therefore in England cannot be more than fixteen millions, which is four millions lefs than the amount of the taxes. But admitting there to be fixteen millions, not more than a fourth part thereof (four millions) can be in London, when it is confidered that every city, town, village, and farm-houfe in the nation muft have a part of it, and that all the great manufactories, which moft require cafh, are out of London. Of this four millions in London, every banker, merchant, tradefman, in fhort every individual muft have fome. He muft be a poor fhop-keeper indeed, who has not a few guineas in his till.

The

The quantity of cafh therefore in the bank can never, on the evidence of circumftances, be fo much as two millions; moft probably not more than one million; and on this flender twig, always liable to be broken, hangs the whole funding fyf-tem of four hundred millions, befides many millions in bank notes. The fum in the bank is not fufficient to pay one-fourth of only one year's inte-reft of the national debt, were the creditors to de-mand payment in cafh, or to demand cafh for the bank-notes in which the intereft is paid. A cir-cumftance always liable to happen.

One of the amufements that has kept up the farce of the funding fyftem is, that the intereft is regularly paid. But as the intereft is always paid in bank notes, and as bank notes can always be coined for the purpofe, this mode of payment proves nothing. The point of proof is, can the bank give cafh for the bank notes on which the intereft is paid? If it cannot, and it is evident it cannot, fome millions of bank notes muft go with-out payment, and thofe holders of bank notes who apply laft will be worft off. When the prefent quantity of cafh in the bank be paid away, it is next to impoffible to fee how any new quantity is to arrive. None will arrive from taxes, for the taxes will all be paid in bank notes; and fhould the government refufe bank notes in payment of

taxes,

taxes, the credit of bank notes will be gone at once. No cafh will arrive from the bufinefs of difcounting merchants bills; for every merchant will pay off thofe bills in bank notes, and not in cafh. There is therefore no means left for the bank to obtain a new fupply of cafh, after the prefent quantity be paid away. But, befides the impoffibility of paying the intereft of the funded debt in cafh, there are many thoufand perfons in London and in the country, who are holders of bank notes that came into their hands in the fair way of trade, and who are not ftock-holders in the funds; and as fuch perfons have had no hand in increafing the demand upon the bank, as thofe have had who, for their own private intereft, like Boyd and others, are contracting, or pretending to contract, for new loans, they will conceive they have a juft right their bank notes fhould be paid firft. Boyd has been very fly in France, in changing his paper into cafh. He will be juft as fly in doing the fame thing in London; for he has learned to calculate : and then it is probable he will fet off for America.

A ftoppage of payment at the bank is not a new thing. Smith, in his Wealth of Nations, book 2, chap. 2, fays, that in the year 1696, exchequer bills fell forty, fifty, and fixty per cent. bank notes twenty per cent, and the bank ftopt payment.——

That

That which happened in 1696 may happen again in 1796. The period in which it happened was the laft year of the war of king William. It neceffarily put a ftop to the further emiffion of exchequer and navy Bills, and to the raifing of new loans; and the peace which took place the next year was probably hurried on by this circumftance, and faved the bank from bankruptcy. Smith, in fpeaking of the circumftances of the bank, upon another occafion, fays (book 2, chap. 2,)—" This " great company has been reduced to the neceffity " of paying in fixpences." When a bank adopts the expedient of paying in fixpences, it is a confeffion of infolvency.

It is worthy of obfervation, that every cafe of a failure in finances, fince the fyftem of paper began, has produced a revolution in governments, either total or partial. A failure in the finances of France produced the French revolution. A failure in the finance of the affignats broke up the revolutionary government, and produced the prefent French Conftitution. A failure in the finances of the old Congrefs of America, and the embarraffments it brought upon commerce, broke up the fyftem of the old confederation, and produced the prefent federal conftitution. If then we admit of reafoning by comparifon of caufes and events, a failure in the
Englifh

English finances will produce some change in the government of that country.

As to Mr. Pitt's project of paying off the national debt by applying a million a year for that purpose, while he continues adding more than twenty millions a year to it, it is like setting a man with a wooden leg to run after a hare. The longer he runs the farther he is off.

When I said that the funding system had entered the last twenty years of its existence, I certainly did not mean that it would continue twenty years, and then expire as a lease would do. I meant to describe that age of decrepitude in which death is every day to be expected, and life cannot continue long. But the death of credit, or that state that is called bankruptcy, is not always marked by those progressive stages of visible decline, that mark the decline of natural life. In the progression of natural life, age cannot counterfeit youth, nor conceal the departure of juvenile abilities. But it is otherwise with respect to the death of credit; for though all the approaches to bankruptcy may actually exist in circumstances, they admit of being concealed by appearances. Nothing is more common than to see the bankrupt of to-day a man in credit but the day before; yet no sooner is the real state of his affairs known, than every body can see he had been insolvent long before. In London, the greatest

theatre

theatre of bankruptcy in Europe, this part of the fubject will be well and feelingly underftood.

Mr. Pitt continually talks of credit, and of the national refources. Thefe are two of the feigned appearances by which the approaches to bankruptcy are concealed. That which he calls credit may exift, as I have juft fhewn, in a ftate of infolvency, and is always what I have before defcribed it to be, *fufpicion afleep.*

As to national refources, Mr. Pitt, like all the Englifh financiers that preceded him fince the funding fyftem began, has uniformly miftaken the nature of a refource; that is, they have miftaken it confiftently with the delufion of the funding fyftem; but time is explaining the delufion. That which he calls, and which they called, a refource, is not a refource, but is the *anticipation* of a refource. They have anticipated what *would have been* a refource in another generation, had not the ufe of it been fo anticipated. The funding fyftem is a fyftem of anticipation. Thofe who eftablifhed it an hundred years ago, anticipated the refources of thofe who were to live an hundred years after; for the people of the prefent day have to pay the intereft of the debts contracted at that time, and of all debts contracted fince. But it is the laft feather that breaks the horfe's back. Had the fyftem began an hundred years before, the amount of

taxes

taxes at this time to pay the annual intereſt at four per cent. (could we ſuppoſe ſuch a ſyſtem of inſanity could have continued) would be two hundred and twenty millions annually ; for the capital of the debt would be 5456 millions, according to the ratio that aſcertains the expence of the wars for the hundred years that are paſt. But long before it could have reached this period, the value of bank notes, from the immenſe quantity of them, (for it is in paper only that ſuch a nominal revenue could be collected) would have been as low or lower than continental paper money has been in America, or aſſignats in France ; and as to the idea of exchanging them for gold and ſilver, it is too abſurd to be contradicted.

Do we not ſee that nature, in all her operations, diſowns the viſionary baſis upon which the funding ſyſtem is built ? She acts always by renewed ſucceſſions, and never by accumulating additions perpetually progreſſing. Animals and vegetables, men and trees, have exiſted ever ſince the world began ; but that exiſtence has been carried on by ſucceſſions of generations, and not by continuing the ſame men and the ſame trees in exiſtence that exiſted firſt ; and to make room for the new ſhe removes the old. Every natural ideot can ſee this. It is the ſtock-jobbing ideot only that miſtakes. He has conceived that art can do what nature can-

not.

not. He is teaching her a new fyftem—that there is no occafion for man to die—That the fcheme of creation can be carried on upon the plan of the funding fyftem—That it can proceed by continual additions of new beings, like new loans, and all live together in eternal youth. Go, count the graves, thou ideot, and learn the folly of thy arithmetic.

But befides thefe things, there is fomething vifibly farcical in the whole operation of loaning. It is fcarcely more than four years ago that fuch a rot of bankruptcy fpread itfelf over London, that the whole commercial fabric tottered ; trade and credit were at a ftand ; and fuch was the ftate of things, that to prevent, or fufpend, a general bankruptcy, the government lent the merchants fix millions in *government* paper, and now the merchants lend the government twenty-two millions in *their* paper; and two parties, Boyd and Morgan, men but little known, contend who fhall be the lenders. What a farce is this ! It reduces the operation of loaning to accommodation paper, in which the competitors contend, not who fhall lend, but who fhall fign, becaufe there is fomething to be got for figning.

Every Englifh ftock-jobber and minifter boafts of the credit of England. Its credit, fay they, is greater than that of any country in Europe. There is a good reafon for this ; for there is not another coun-

try

try in Europe that could be made the dupe of fuch a delufion. The Englifh funding fyftem will remain a monument of wonder, not fo much on account of the extent to which it has been carried, as of the folly of believing in it.

Thofe who had formerly predicted that the funding fyftem would break up when the debt fhould amount to one hundred or one hundred and fifty millions, erred only in not diftinguifhing between infolvency and actual bankruptcy; for the infolvency commenced as foon as the government became unable to pay the intereft in cafh, or to give cafh for the bank notes in which the intereft was paid, whether that inability was known or not, or whether it was fufpected or not. Infolvency always takes place before bankruptcy; for bankruptcy is nothing more than the publication of that infolvency. In the affairs of an individual, it often happens that infolvency exifts feveral years before bankruptcy, and that the infolvency is concealed and carried on till the individual is not able to pay one fhilling in the pound. A government can ward off bankruptcy longer than an individual; but infolvency will inevitably produce bankruptcy, whether in an individual or in a government. If then the quantity of bank notes payable on demand, which the bank has iffued, are greater than the bank can pay off,

off, the bank is infolvent; and when that infolvency be declared, it is bankruptcy.*

I come

* Among the delufions that have been impofed upon the nation by minifters, to give a falfe coloring to its affairs, and by none more than by Mr. Pitt, is a motley, amphibious cha-raftered thing called the *balance of trade.* This balance of trade, as it is called, is taken from the cuftom-houfe books, in which entries are made of all cargoes exported, and alfo of all cargoes imported, in each year; and when the value of the exports, according to the price fet upon them by the exporter or by the cuftom-houfe, is greater than the value of the imports, eftimated in the fame manner, they fay, the balance of trade is fo much in their favor.

The cuftom-houfe books prove regularly enough that fo many cargoes have been exported, and fo many imported; but this is all that they prove, or were intended to prove. They have nothing to do with the balance of profit or lofs; and it is ignorance to appeal to them upon that account: for the cafe is, that the greater the lofs is in any one year, the higher will this thing called the balance of trade appear to be according to the cuftom-houfe books. For example, nearly the whole of the Mediterranean convoy has been taken by the French this year; confequently thofe cargoes will not appear as imports on the cuftom-houfe books, and therefore the balance of trade, by which they mean the pro-fits of it, will appear to be fo much the greater as the lofs amounts to; and, on the other hand, had the lofs not hap-pened, the profits would have appeared to have been fo much the lefs. All the loffes happening at fea to returning cargoes, by accidents, by the elements, or by capture, make the ba-lance appear the higher on the fide of the exports; and were

they

I come now to fhew the feveral ways by which bank notes get into circulation. I fhall afterwards offer an eftimate on the total quantity or amount of bank notes exifting at this moment.

The bank acts in three capacities. As a bank of difcount; as a bank of depofit; and as banker for the government.

Firft, as a bank of difcount. The bank difcounts merchants bills of exchange for two months. When a merchant has a bill that will become due at the end of two months, and wants payment before that time, the bank advances that payment to him, deducting therefrom at the rate of five per cent. per ann. The bill of exchange remains at the bank as a pledge or pawn, and at the end of two months it muft be redeemed. This tranfaction is done altogether in paper; for the profits of the bank, as a

they all loft at fea, it would appear to be all profit on the cuftom-houfe books. Alfo every cargo of exports that is loft that occafions another to be fent, adds in like manner to the fide of the exports, and appears as profit. This year the balance of trade will appear high, becaufe the lofles have been great by capture and by ftorms. The ignorance of the Britifh Parliament, in liftening to this hackneyed impofition of minifters about the balance of trade, is aftonifhing. It fhews how little they know of national affairs; and Mr. Grey may as well talk Greek to them, as make motions about the ftate of the nation. They underftand fox-hunting and the game-laws.

bank

bank of difcount, arife entirely from its making ufe of paper as money. The bank gives bank notes to the merchant in difcounting the bill of exchange, and the redeemer of the bill pays bank notes to the bank in redeeming it. It very feldom happens that any real money paffes between them.

If the profits of a bank be, for example, two hundred thoufand pounds a year (a great fum to be made merely by exchanging one fort of paper for another, and which fhews alfo that the merchants of that place are preffed for money for payments, inftead of having money to fpare to lend to government), it proves that the bank difcounts to the amount of four millions annually, or 666,666l. every two months; and as there never remain in the bank more than two months pledges, of the value of 666,666l. at any one time, the amount of bank notes in circulation at any one time fhould not be more than to that amount. This is fufficient to fhew that the prefent immenfe quantity of bank notes, which are diftributed through every city, town, village, and farm-houfe in England, cannot be accounted for on the fcore of difcounting.

Secondly, as a bank of depofit. To depofit money at the bank means to lodge it there for the fake of convenience, and to be drawn out at any moment the depofitor pleafes, or to be paid away to his order. When the bufinefs of difcounting is great, that of

depofiting

depofiting is neceffarily fmall. No man depofits and applies for difcounts at the fame time; for it would be like paying intereft for lending money, inftead of for borrowing it. The depofits that are now made at the bank are almoft entirely in bank notes, and confequently they add nothing to the ability of the bank to pay off the bank notes that may be prefented for payment; and befides this, the depofits are no more the property of the bank than the cafh or bank notes in a merchant's counting houfe are the property of his book-keeper. No great increafe therefore of bank notes, beyond what the difcounting bufinefs admits, can be accounted for on the fcore of depofits.

Thirdly. The bank afts as banker for the government. This is the conneftion that threatens ruin to every public bank. It is through this conneftion that the credit of a bank is forced far beyond what it ought to be, and ftill further beyond its ability to pay. It is through this conneftion that fuch an immenfe redundant quantity of bank notes have gotten into circulation; and which, inftead of being iffued becaufe there was property in the bank, have been iffued becaufe there was none.

When the treafury is empty, which happens in almoft every year of every war, its coffers at the bank are empty alfo. It . in this condition of emptinefs that the minifter has recourfe to emiffions

of what are called exchequer and navy bills, which
continually generates a new increase of bank notes,
and which are sported upon the public without
there being property in the bank to pay them.—
These exchequer and navy bills (being, as I have
said, emitted because the treasury and its coffers at
the bank are empty, and cannot pay the demands
that come in) are no other than an acknowledgement
that the bearer is entitled to receive so much money. They may be compared to the settlement
of an account, in which the debtor acknowledges
the balance he owes, and for which he gives a note
of hand ; or to a note of hand given to raise money
upon it.

Sometimes the bank discounts those bills as it
would discount merchants bills of exchange ; sometimes it purchases them of the holders at the cur-
rent price ; and sometimes it agrees with the minister to pay an interest upon them to the holders,
and keep them in circulation. In every one of
those cases an additional quantity of bank notes
get into circulation, and are sported, as I have said,
upon the public, without there being property in
the bank, as banker for the government, to pay
them : and besides this, the bank has now no money
of its own ; for the money that was originally sub-
scribed to begin the credit of the bank with at its
firſt

firſt eſtabliſhment, has been lent to government, and waſted long ago.

" The bank (ſays Smith, book 2, chap. 2,) aɛts " not only as an ordinary bank, but as a great en- " gine of ſtate; it receives and pays the greater " part of the annuities which are due to the cre- " ditors of the *public.*" (It is worth obſerving, that the *public,* or the *nation,* is always put for the government in ſpeaking of debts.) " It circulates (ſays Smith) " exchequer bills, and it advances to " government the annual amount of the land and " malt taxes, which are frequently not paid till " feveral years afterwards." (This advancement is alſo done in bank notes, for which there is not property in the bank.) " In thoſe different ope- " rations, (ſays Smith) *its duty to the public* may " fometimes have obliged it, without any fault of " its directors, *to overſlock the circulation with paper* " *money,*"—bank notes. How its *duty to the public* can induce it *to overſlock that public* with promiſ- fory bank notes which it *cannot pay,* and thereby expofe the individuals of that public to ruin, is too paradoxical to be explained; for it is on the credit which individuals *give to the bank,* by receiving and circulating its notes, and not upon its *own* credit or its *own* property, for it has none, that the bank ſports. If however it be the duty of the bank to expofe the public to this hazard, it is at leaſt equally

the

the duty of the individuals of that public to get
their money and take care of themfelves; and leave
it to placemen, penfioners, government contractors,
Reeves's affociation, and the members of both
houfes of Parliament, who have voted away the
money at the nod of the minifter, to continue the
credit if they can, and for which their eftates individually and collectively ought to anfwer, as far
as they will go.

There has always exifted, and ftill exifts, a myf-
terious, fufpicious connection, between the minifter
and the directors of the bank, and which explains
itfelf no otherways than by a continual increafe of
bank notes. Without, therefore, entering into any
further details of the various contrivances by which
bank notes are iffued, and thrown upon the public,
I proceed, as I before mentioned, to offer an eftimate on the total quantity of bank notes in circulation.

However difpofed governments may be to wring
money by taxes from the people, there is a limit to
the practice eftablifhed in the nature of things. That
limit is the proportion between the quantity of money in a nation, be that quantity what it may, and
the greateft quantity of taxes that can be raifed
upon it. People have other ufes for money befides
paying taxes; and it is only a proportional part of
that money they can fpare for taxes, as it is only a
pro-

proportional part they can fpare for houfe-rent, for clothing, or for any other particular ufe. Thefe proportions find out and eftablifh themfelves; and that with fuch exactnefs, that if any one part exceeds its proportion, all the other parts feel it.

Before the invention of paper money (bank notes), there was no other money in the nation than gold and filver, and the greateft quantity of money that ever was raifed in taxes during that period, never exceeded a fourth part of the quantity of money in the nation. It was high taxing when it came to this point. The taxes in the time of William the Third never reached to four millions before the invention of paper, and the quantity of money in the nation at that time was eftimated to be about fixteen millions. The fame proportions eftablifhed themfelves in France. There was no paper money in France before the prefent revolution, and the taxes were collected in gold and filver money. The higheft quantity of taxes never exceeded twenty-two millions fterling; and the quantity of gold and filver money in the nation at the fame time, as ftated by Mr. Neckar, from returns of coinage at the mints, in his Treatife on the Adminiftration of the Finances, was about ninety millions fterling. To go beyond this limit of a fourth part, in England, they were obliged to introduce paper money; and the attempt to go beyond it in France,

where

where paper could not be introduced, broke up the government. This proportion therefore of a fourth part, is the limit which the nature of the thing establishes for itself, be the quantity of money in a nation more or lefs.

The amount of taxes in England at this time is full twenty millions; and therefore the quantity of gold and filver, and of bank notes, taken together, amounts to eighty millions. The quantity of gold and filver, as stated by Lord Hawkesbury's secretary (George Chalmers), as I have before fhewn, is twenty millions; and therefore the total amount of bank notes in circulation, all made payable on demand, is fixty millions. This enormous fum will aftonifh the moft ftupid flock-jobber, and overpower the credulity of the moft thoughtlefs Englifhman : but were it only a third part of that fum, the bank cannot pay half a crown in the pound.

There is fomething curious in the movements of this modern complicated machine, the funding fyftem; and it is only now that it is beginning to unfold the full extent of its movements. In the firft part of its movements it gives great powers into the hands of government, and in the laft part it takes them completely away.

The funding fyftem fet out with raifing revenues under the name of loans, by means of which government became both prodigal and powerful.

The

The loaners affumed the name of creditors, and though it was foon difcovered that loaning was government jobbing, thofe pretended loaners, or the perfons who purchafed into the funds afterwards, conceived themfelves not only to be creditors, but to be the *only* creditors.

But fuch has been the operation of this complicated machine, the funding fyftem, that it has produced, unperceived, a fecond generation of creditors, more numerous and far more formidable, and withal more real than the firft generation ; for every holder of a bank note is a creditor, and a real creditor, and the debt due to him is made payable on demand. The debt therefore which the government owes to individuals is compofed of two parts; the one about four hundred millions bearing intereft, the other about fixty millions payable on demand. The one is called the funded debt, the other is the debt due in bank notes.

This fecond debt (that contained in the bank notes) has, in a great meafure, been incurred to pay the intereft of the firft debt; fo that in fact little or no real intereft has been paid by government. The whole has been delufion and fraud. Government firft contracted a debt in the form of loans with one clafs of people, and then run clandeftinely into debt with another clafs, by means of bank notes. to pay the intereft. Government acted

of

of itſelf in contracting the firſt debt, and made a machine of the bank to contract the ſecond.

It is this ſecond debt that changes the ſeat of power and the order of things; for it puts it in the power of even a ſmall part of the holders of bank-notes (had they no other motive than diſguſt at Pitt and Grenville's ſedition bills) to controul any meaſure of government they found to be injurious to their intereſt; and that not by popular meetings, or popular ſocieties, but by the ſimple and eaſy operation of with-holding their credit from that government; that is, by individually demanding payment at the bank for every bank-note that comes into their hands. Why ſhould Pitt and Grenville expect that the very men whom they in-ſult and injure ſhould at the ſame time continue to ſupport the meaſures of Pitt and Grenville, by giving credit to their promiſſory notes of payment? No new emiſſions of bank-notes could go on while payment was demanding on the old and the caſh in the bank waſting daily away; nor any new ad-vances be made to government or to the emperor to carry on the war; nor any new emiſſion be made of exchequer bills.

" *The bank*," ſays Smith, (book ii. ch. 2.) " is " *a great engine of ſtate.*" And in the ſame para-graph he ſays, " *The ſtability of the bank is equal* " *to that of the Britiſh government;*" which is the

ſame

fame as to fay that the ftability of the government
is equal to that of the bank, and no more. If then
the bank cannot pay, the *arch-treafurer of the holy
Roman empire* (S. R. I. A.*) is a bankrupt. When
Folly invented titles, fhe did not attend to their
application; for ever fince the government of England has been in the hands of *arch-treafurers*, it has
been running into bankruptcy; and as to the arch-
treafurer *apparent*, he has been a bankrupt long
ago. What a miferable profpect has England before its eyes!

Before the war of 1755 there were no bank notes
lower than twenty pounds. During that war bank
notes of fifteen pounds and of ten pounds were
coined; and now, fince the commencement of the
prefent war, they are coined as low as five pounds.
Thefe five pounds notes will circulate chiefly among
little fhop keepers, butchers, bakers, market people, renters of fmall houfes, lodgers, &c. All the
high departments of commerce, and the affluent
ftations of life were already *overftocked*, as Smith
expreffes it, with the bank notes. No place re-
mained open wherein to crowd an additional quantity of bank notes but among the clafs of people I
have juft mentioned, and the means of doing this
could be beft effected by coining five pound notes.
This conduct has the appearance of that of an un-

* Part of the infcription on an Englifh guinea.

E   prin-

principled infolvent who, when on the verge of
bankruptcy to the amount of many thoufands, will
borrow as low as five pounds of the fervants in his
houfe, and break the next day.

But whatever momentary relief or aid the minifter and his bank might expeft from this low con-
trivance of five pound notes, it will increafe the
inability of the bank to pay the higher notes, and
haften the deftruftion of all; for even the fmall
taxes that ufed to be paid in money will now be
paid in thofe notes, and the bank will foon find itfelf with fcarcely any other money than what the
hair powder guinea tax brings in.

The bank notes make the moft ferious part of
the bufinefs of finance; what is called the national
funded debt is but a trifle when put in comparifon
with it; yet the cafe of the bank notes has never
been touched upon. But it certainly ought to be
known upon what authority, whether that of the
minifter or of the direftors, and upon what foun-
dation, fuch immenfe quantities are iffued. I have
ftated the amount of them at fixty millions fterling; I have produced data for that eftimation;
and befides this, the apparent quantity of them, far
beyond that of gold and filver in the nation, corro-
borates therewith. But were there but a third
part of fixty millions, the bank cannot pay half a
crown in the pound; for no new fupply of money,

as

as before faid, can arrive at the bank, as all the taxes will be paid in paper.

When the funding fyftem began, it was not doubted that the loans that had been borrowed would be repaid. Government not only propagated that belief, but it began paving them off. In time this prot. Tion came to be abandoned; and it is not difficult to fee that bank notes will march the fame way; for the amount of them is only another debt under another name; and the probability is, that Mr. Pitt will at laft propofe funding them. In that cafe bank notes will not be fo valuable as French affignats. The affignats have a folid property in referve in the national domains; bank notes have none; and befides this, the Englifh revenue muft then fink down to what the amount of it was before the funding fyftem began; between three and four millions. One of which the *arch-treafurer* would require for himfelf, and the arch-treafurer *apparent* would require three quarters of a million more to pay his debts. " *In* " *France*," fays Sterne, " *they order thefe things* " *better*."

I have now expofed the Englifh fyftem of finance to the eyes of all nations; for this work will be publifhed in all languages. In doing this, I have done an act of juftice to thofe numerous citizens of neutral nations who have been impofed

upon

upon by that fraudulent fyftem, and who have property at ftake upon the event.

As an individual citizen of America, and as far as an individual can go, I have revenged (if I may ufe the expreffion without any immoral meaning) the p'ratical depredations committed on the American commerce by the Englifh government.—I have retaliated for France on the fubject of finance; and I conclude with retorting on Mr. Pitt the expreffion he ufed againft France, and fay, that the Englifh fyftem of finance " IS ON THE VERGE, " NAY EVEN IN THE GULPH OF BANKRUPTCY."

THOMAS PAINE.

Paris, 19th Germinal,
4th year of the Republic.
April 8, 1796.

www.ingramcontent.com/pod-product-compliance
Lightning Source LLC
Chambersburg PA
CBHW030710110426
42739CB00031B/1522